Table of Contents

Completing the Team Leadership
Questionnaire (TLQ) involves 5 steps.

Step 1: *(5 minutes)*
Read the Introduction to Leadership

Step 2: *(10 minutes)*
Complete the Questionnaire

Step 3: *(10 minutes)*
Score yourself

Step 4: *(15 minutes)*
Read about team leadership

Step 5: *(30 minutes to 1 hour)*
Develop a leadership plan

Objectives

After completing this questionnaire you will:

- Understand the 3 dimensions of team leadership
- Understand the importance of learning in team leadership
- Identify your strengths in leading a team on 8 key leadership beliefs and behaviors
- Create a leadership plan

Who Should Use This Questionnaire?

A variety of team leaders will find the TLQ a valuable resource to describe their team leadership style. The questionnaire is most useful for those who already have experience as a formal leader. However, those new to a formal leadership role will also find the questionnaire helpful in developing team leadership skills.

A team exists anytime people must work together to accomplish a task. Leaders involved in many different types of teams will find the team leader questionnaire useful.

- Teams involved in education, development, and training courses
- Work teams
- Project teams and task forces
- Virtual teams
- Self-directed teams

STEP 1:
INTRODUCTION TO TEAM LEADERSHIP

· ·

Team leadership is the process where a leader helps a team improve the way it solves problems and gets work done.

This questionnaire will help you 1) assess your knowledge, skills and abilities as a team leader and 2) continue to improve your team's effectiveness.

The Team Leadership Questionnaire helps team leaders assess their own beliefs and behaviors in teams. This booklet also provides a comprehensive study guide to improving team leadership skills and producing more effective teams.

The Team Leadership Questionnaire focuses on how leaders act and perceive their actions in a team environment. Knowing more about your perceived strengths and weaknesses will improve your ability to lead a team in:

1. Solving problems
2. Learning from errors and mistakes
3. Setting goals
4. Working together to achieve goals
5. Building trust among members
6. Building confidence as a team
7. Drawing on the strengths of individual team members
8. Coordinate knowledge and actions between team members

STEP 2:
COMPLETE THE QUESTIONNAIRE

Instructions

The Team Leadership Questionnaire measures your team leadership style. There are no right or wrong answers. Your honest response to these questions will assist in accurately identifying your skills.

The first step in improving a team's function and enhancing its effectiveness is to understand how team leadership can facilitate this process.

On the following page are statements a person might say about his or her leadership actions. Indicate how accurate or inaccurate each statement is by circling how well each statement describes your actions or beliefs leading a team.

Please be sure to complete both Sections I and II. Once you complete both sections, you will score your responses and be able to compare your scores to the average scores of other team leaders.

SECTION I: *Circle a number representing how accurately each sentence ending reflects your actions or beliefs as a team leader.*

1	2	3	4	5	6	7
Very Inaccurate	Mostly Inaccurate	Slightly Inaccurate	Neutral	Slightly Accurate	Mostly Accurate	Very Accurate

When leading a team I . . .

	Very Inaccurate						Very Accurate
1. encourage members to share different opinions.	1	2	3	4	5	6	7
2. take time in team meetings to "check in with" each member to see how things are going.	1	2	3	4	5	6	7
3. know the specific areas of expertise of my members.	1	2	3	4	5	6	7
4. believe that team members typically share a common purpose.	1	2	3	4	5	6	7
5. can give others feedback without them being offended.	1	2	3	4	5	6	7
6. know when a team member is having a bad day.	1	2	3	4	5	6	7
7. understand the unique work performed by my team members.	1	2	3	4	5	6	7
8. generally focus on the team success more than any one individual's success.	1	2	3	4	5	6	7
9. support my team members when they say something that may be seen as unpopular.	1	2	3	4	5	6	7
10. know when individual team members are under stress.	1	2	3	4	5	6	7

	Very Inaccurate						Very Accurate
11. make sure we have clearly divided tasks.	1	2	3	4	5	6	7
12. share the same goals as my team members.	1	2	3	4	5	6	7
13. encourage my team members to express many different viewpoints.	1	2	3	4	5	6	7
14. aware of the feelings and moods of my team members at each meeting.	1	2	3	4	5	6	7
15. know who is best at what assigned tasks.	1	2	3	4	5	6	7
16. recognize how individual goals fit in with team goals.	1	2	3	4	5	6	7
17. think it is unacceptable for other team members to challenge my viewpoint.	1	2	3	4	5	6	7
18. don't pay attention to individual mood swings.	1	2	3	4	5	6	7
19. am unaware of the strengths and weaknesses of team members.	1	2	3	4	5	6	7
20. focus on meeting individual member goals rather than the team goals.	1	2	3	4	5	6	7
21. know when members trust each other.	1	2	3	4	5	6	7
22. understand when a team member is in a bad mood.	1	2	3	4	5	6	7
23. create a clear division of labor among team members.	1	2	3	4	5	6	7
24. understand the individual goals of my team members.	1	2	3	4	5	6	7

Please continue to Section II.

SECTION II: *How accurately does this statement reflect what you do as a team leader?*

1	2	3	4	5	6	7
Very Inaccurate	Mostly Inaccurate	Slightly Inaccurate	Neutral	Slightly Accurate	Mostly Accurate	Very Accurate

When I am leading a team,
 my team members . . .

                     Very Inaccurate   Very Accurate

25. typically can solve any issues they come up against.   1 2 3 4 5 6 7

26. work on their project individually, but keep other team members informed on progress.   1 2 3 4 5 6 7

27. know what to do when faced with an unexpected problem.   1 2 3 4 5 6 7

28. make sure that experienced team members share their knowledge with less experienced team members.   1 2 3 4 5 6 7

29. know they can accomplish anything.   1 2 3 4 5 6 7

30. keep up-to-date on the progress of team projects.   1 2 3 4 5 6 7

31. can respond to new issues as they arise.   1 2 3 4 5 6 7

32. find several alternative ways to solve a problem.   1 2 3 4 5 6 7

33. often face roadblocks that they don't know how to deal with.   1 2 3 4 5 6 7

34. step in when other team members have a problem.   1 2 3 4 5 6 7

35. help the team so that when it faces a tense situation, they know how to react.   1 2 3 4 5 6 7

TEAM LEADERSHIP QUESTIONNAIRE

	Very Inaccurate					Very Accurate
36. find and correct possible mistakes before they happen.	1	2	3	4	5	6	7
37. believe they will be successful.	1	2	3	4	5	6	7
38. coordinate their work with one another.	1	2	3	4	5	6	7
39. know what to do if something goes wrong.	1	2	3	4	5	6	7
40. evaluate team process and procedures.	1	2	3	4	5	6	7
41. are often uncertain about whether or not they will be successful.	1	2	3	4	5	6	7
42. never know what other members are going to do.	1	2	3	4	5	6	7
43. are confident that they will perform well.	1	2	3	4	5	6	7
44. often repeat the same mistakes several times.	1	2	3	4	5	6	7
45. believe they will perform better than other teams.	1	2	3	4	5	6	7
46. ensure that the team works together without thinking too hard about it.	1	2	3	4	5	6	7
47. discuss ways to deal with setbacks.	1	2	3	4	5	6	7
48. seek to improve themselves as team members.	1	2	3	4	5	6	7

Now continue to Step 3 to score your responses.

STEP 3:
SCORE YOURSELF

. . . .

Total Items:

1	1, 5, 9, 13, 21	=	_____	(*Total Score on* **Psychological Safety**)
2	2, 6, 10, 14, 22	=	_____	(*Total Score on* **Interpersonal Understanding**)
3	3, 7, 11, 15, 23	=	_____	(*Total Score on* **Team Roles**)
4	4, 8, 12, 16, 24	=	_____	(*Total Score on* **Goals**)
5	25, 29, 43, 37, 45	=	_____	(*Total Score on* **Confidence**)
6	26, 30, 34, 38, 46	=	_____	(*Total Score on* **Coordinating**)
7	28, 32, 36, 40, 48	=	_____	(*Total Score on* **Continuous Improvement**)
8	27, 31, 35, 39, 47	=	_____	(*Total Score on* **Adapting**)

PLOT YOUR SCORES

Now that you have found your individual scores, you can compare your scores to a sample of leaders. Using your scores from the prior page, now plot your score on the corresponding dimension below.

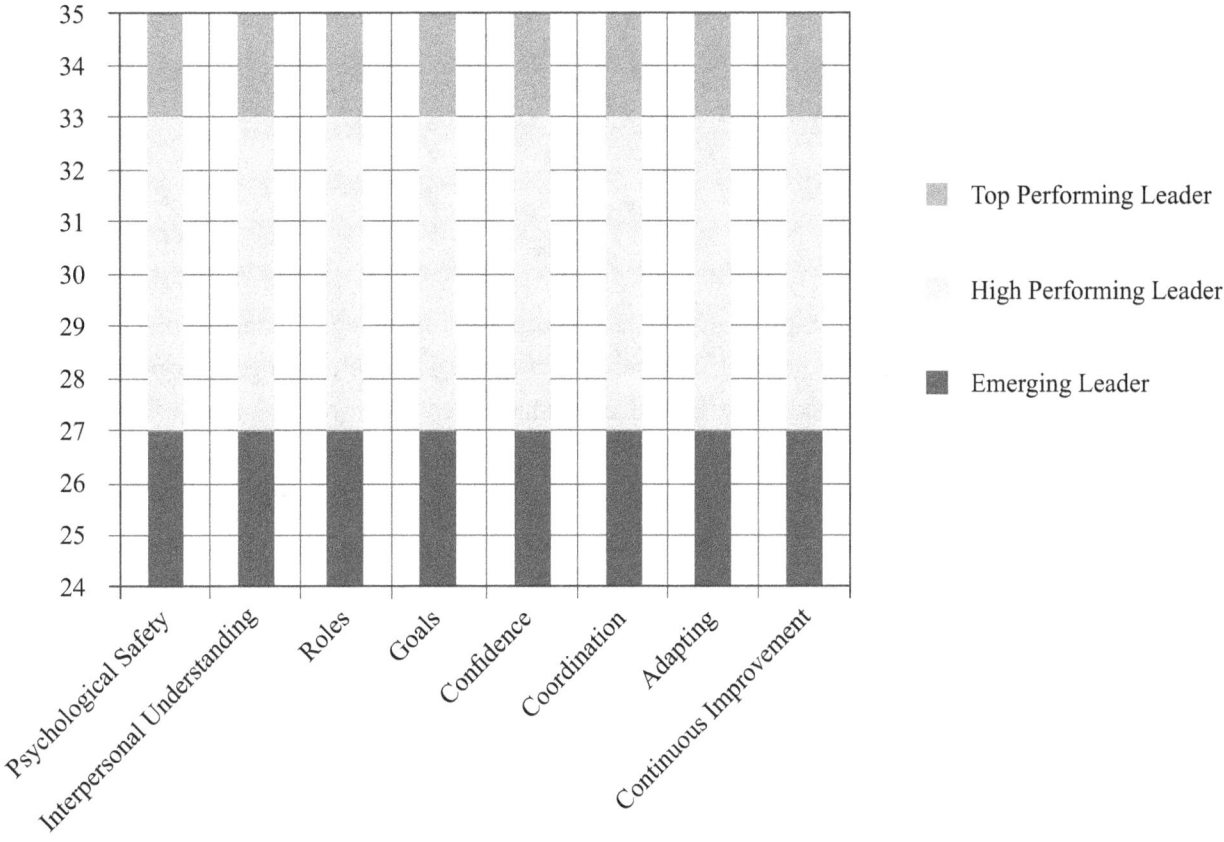

Top Performing Leader

High Performing Leader

Emerging Leader

STEP 3 (CONTINUED):
INTERPRETING YOUR SCORES

. . . .

Classifying your scores

Look at your scores compared to the sample scores listed on the previous page. When you place your scores on the graph, you are comparing yourself to a sample of about 1,000 emerging, high-performing, and top-performing leaders who have taken the Team Leadership Questionnaire.

Your scores will place you in one of three leadership categories for each of the eight team leadership dimensions:

Top performing leader. You have evaluated your skill as a top performing team leader. This means that you see yourself as among the top performing leaders. As a top-performing leader you regularly facilitate learning and build specific behaviors and beliefs.

High performing leader. You have evaluated your skill as a high performing team leader. This means you see yourself as an effective team leader. As a high performing leader you are able to facilitate a specific belief and behavior into your role as a team leader.

Emerging leader. You have evaluated your skill as an emerging leader. This means you see yourself as ready to begin building your team leadership skills by integrating learning beliefs and behaviors into your team leadership.

Comparing Your Scores

Now that you have compared your scores to the sample of other leaders, now take a moment to compare your scores along the eight dimensions of team leadership.

Answer the following questions based on the sample scores compared with your scores:

- What are your top three strongest areas as a team leader?

    1. _____

    2. _____

    3. _____

- What are your bottom three areas as a team leader?

    1. _____

    2. _____

    3. _____

STEP 4:
READ ABOUT TEAM LEADERSHIP
. . . .

The Critical Role of the Team Leader

Team leadership plays a critical role in team performance. Team leadership creates the overall tone of the team, motivates members and sets general direction. The most important part of leadership, however, involves helping team members learn to be more effective contributors to the team. Leadership on teams involves two steps. First, leadership involves creating shared beliefs among team members that foster an environment of learning. Second, leadership requires helping team members improve their teamwork skills.

The TLQ provides a comprehensive view of team leadership based on years of re-search and consulting with hundreds of teams. Mastering team leadership means:

- Increasing your understanding of how teams work
- Coordinating the various components that, when taken together, constitute team effectiveness
- Developing skills that improve your ability to lead a team
- Improving skills of your team members

What is Team Learning?

Team learning involves a variety of shared beliefs and behaviors that lead to improved performance. As teams work together over time, they develop certain patterns. These patterns may be more or less helpful to the team in accomplishing its day-to-day work. Team leadership involves recognizing which learning patterns contribute to the overall success of the team and which patterns get in the way.

These team patterns are often called norms. Norms describe the normal way a team works together.

Norms include:
- The shared beliefs and attitudes among team members.
- The way a team accomplishes its work.
- The way a team goes about solving problems.
- The informal and formal rules a team has about its interactions.

Team Leadership through Learning

Team leadership helps improve team performance by enhancing three key areas:

1. Task Beliefs   *2.* Interpersonal Beliefs   *3.* Team Learning Actions

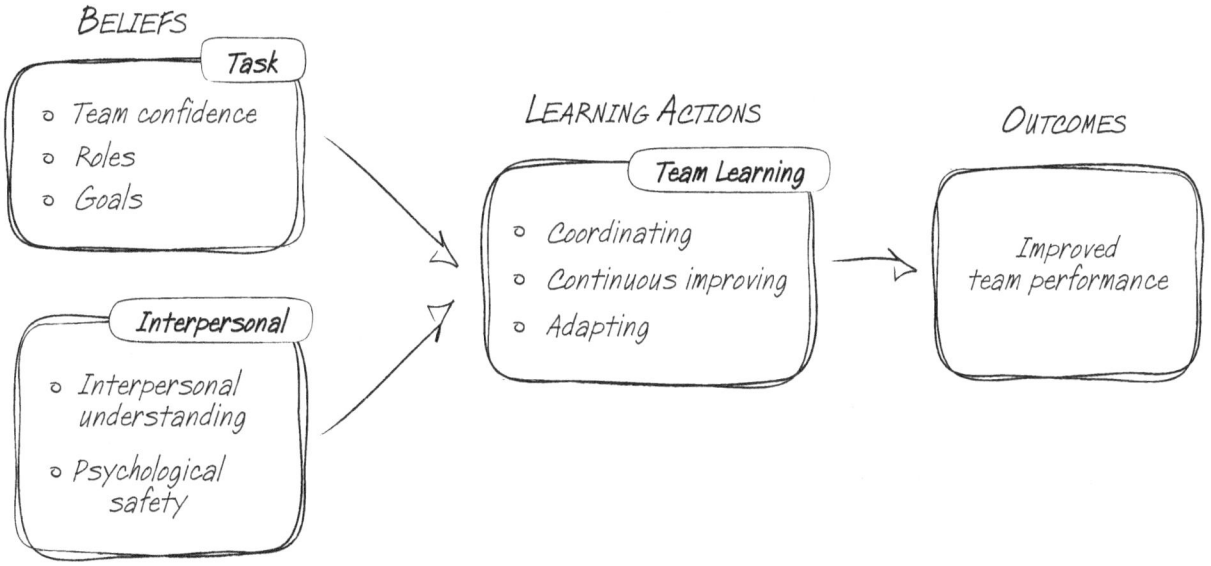

Shared Beliefs

Research shows that when team members share certain beliefs about the nature of their team and teamwork, teams are more likely to learn. The team leader plays a key role in helping establish these patterns of shared beliefs. These shared beliefs can be broken down into two categories, **interpersonal beliefs** and **task beliefs**:

Interpersonal Beliefs

Interpersonal beliefs are the degree to which a team shares beliefs or values related to other team members. These include shared feelings, moods or intentions:

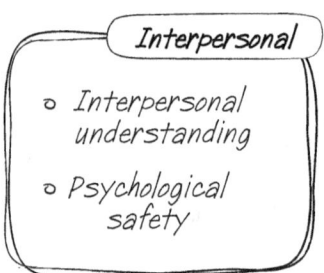

Interpersonal Understanding – the degree to which team members can recognize and comprehend the emotional states, preferences, skills or relationships of individuals in the team.

Psychological Safety – the shared perception by team members about the nature of the team and its members (including the leader) regarding the psychological climate, emotional disposition of the team, and the degree to which members of the team are willing to share sensitive information. Shared information includes people's ability to feel safe to make or admit errors and mistakes, or take challenging or controversial positions without fear of serious repercussions.

Task Beliefs

Task beliefs are the degree to which a team shares beliefs or values related to the task or problem it faces:

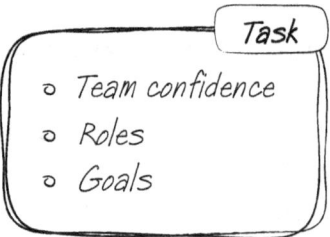

Team Confidence – the team confidence level, in terms of the how strongly the team members share the perception that they can accomplish the task put forth before them.

Roles – the degree to which team members have a distinct division of labor, understand the strengths and weakness of other members, and know the unique skills or tasks assigned to other members.

Goals – the degree to which the team members agree that they have a clear and shared goal or common purpose.

Team Learning Behaviors

Not all teams learn in the same way. In fact, team learning involves three specific ways.

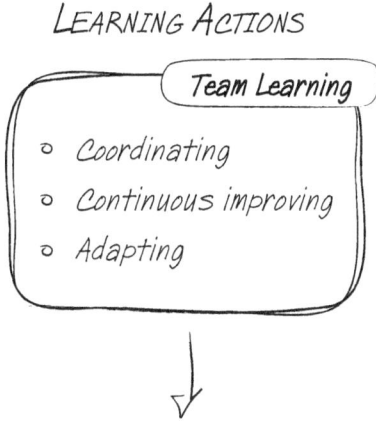

Coordinating – *(How work gets done)*
Team members' ability to get work done through gathering and processing knowledge.

Continuous Improvement – *(Improve how work gets done)*
Team members' ability to improve how they get work done.

Adapting – *(Responding to the unexpected)*
Team members' ability to respond to unexpected and unusual events and still get work done.

Achieving Team Performance through Learning

Taken together shared task beliefs, interpersonal beliefs, and team learning actions provide a comprehensive model for team effectiveness.

Team performance, the outcomes sought by a team can take many forms. Team effectiveness can take many forms.

Teams may seek to:

- ensure quality and safety
- solve problems
- create new knowledge
- improve processes
- develop individual team members

Many teams will have multiple goals such as accomplishing their day-to-day tasks and training or developing the skills of team members. In general, teams are effective when they consider at least four types of outcomes:

Interpersonal Development – the development of interpersonal skills, developing the "emotional intelligence" or the ability of team members to understand one another.

Knowledge Creation – improve critical thinking, responding to problems in new and novel ways and creating knowledge or organizing existing information into usable formats.

Decision Making – making decisions or recommendations to others.

Action – taking multiple actions, or solving a simple problem.

STEP 5:
DEVELOPING A LEADERSHIP PLAN

The next step in developing team leadership skills is to prioritize which areas that you want to work on. It is helpful to pick a couple of areas that you feel are top priority for team leadership. The categories listed below provide some helpful considerations for you to continue to build on your strengths and to develop the areas that you wish.

I wish to build on the following strengths:

_____

_____

_____

_____

I wish to focus my development on the following dimensions of my team:

_____

_____

_____

_____

We have included some strategies that leaders can use to develop the eight areas listed below.

These strategies and others are described in detail in the back of this packet under the **Strategies for Leaders** heading. You can refer to these strategies or devise your own. Describe which strategy you will be utilizing for the areas on which you will be focusing.

INTERPERSONAL BELIEFS

Psychological Safety

- Creating an environment where members of your work team can talk about problems.

  (e.g. How do you communicate with people when they make mistakes?)

- Encouraging different viewpoints.

  (e.g. How do you make sure that all of your team members have an opportunity to express their viewpoints? How do you make sure that one person does not dominate the conversation?)

Your Ideas or refer to "Strategies for Leaders":

_____

_____

_____

_____

_____

_____

Interpersonal Understanding

- Creating an environment where members are aware of the particular situation of individuals, including their current stresses, concerns and demands on their time.

- Encouraging a "check in" at each meeting where individuals bring to light particular issues faced by team members

Your Ideas or refer to "Strategies for Leaders":

_____

_____

_____

_____

_____

_____

TASK BELIEFS

Goals

- Making sure that team members share the same goals.

- Ensuring that team members place the common goals above any individual goals

(e.g. How do I make sure that team members share a common purpose?)

Your Ideas or refer to "Strategies for Leaders":

_____
_____
_____
_____
_____
_____

Team Confidence

- Ensuring that team members feel confident that they can accomplish their work tasks.

(e.g. How do I build the confidence of all of my team members?)

- Making sure that team members feel that they can solve any task related issues that they encounter.

Your Ideas or refer to "Strategies for Leaders":

_____
_____
_____
_____

Roles

- Team members know the expertise and experience of other members.
- The team has a clear division of labor.
- Assigned tasks to individuals that contribute to the team goal.

Your Ideas or refer to "Strategies for Leaders":

_____
_____
_____

TEAM LEARNING ACTIONS

Coordinating

- Making sure that I understand the different work that my team members are doing.

- Ensuring that my team members are coordinating tasks among team members.

  (e.g. How do I make sure that my team members are coordinating their work among themselves when necessary?)

- Am I kept informed about the work of the team appropriately?

- What innovations can I encourage for my team to better coordinate its work?

Your Ideas or refer to "Strategies for Leaders":

_____

_____

_____

_____

_____

_____

Continuous Improvement

Solving problems involves the following:

- Making sure all individuals on the team share knowledge, especially those with experience sharing with less experienced members.

- Ensuring that team members seek multiple alternatives when solving problems.

  (e.g. How can I make sure those team members are seeking enough information to accurately and innovatively solve problems?)

- Identifying and correcting mistakes before they happen.

- Evaluating processes and procedures.

Your Ideas or refer to "Strategies for Leaders":

_____

_____

_____

_____

_____

_____

TEAM LEARNING ACTIONS

Adapting

- Ensuring that my team members are flexible to respond to change.

  (e.g. How do I make sure that my team members are flexible?)

- Making sure that my team members are able to change their actions and beliefs when faced with new information.

  (e.g. How do I make sure that my team members can respond to new information when it is presented?)

Your Ideas or refer to "Strategies for Leaders":

_____

_____

_____

_____

_____

_____

QUESTIONS FOR REFLECTION

1. What experiences have I had with team learning?

2. On the teams that I have had experience with, which components of team learning (roles, goals, adapting, etc.) have team members struggled with? Why?

3. Which components of team learning have been easy? Why?

4. What barriers to team learning have I encountered? What is my role as a leader in removing these barriers?

5. Which strategies do I think will be easy? Which will be more difficult?

ABOUT THE TEAM LEADERSHIP QUESTIONNAIRE

The Team Leadership Questionnaire is based on years of research and work with thousands of teams in business, government, military, and higher education. Over the course of a decade, the authors have collected data and observed thousands of team leaders. The result is the Team Learning Questionnaire. It is based on the following ideas:

- Team learning is the basis for team effectiveness
- Team learning requires certain Knowledge, Skills and Abilities (KSAs)
- Assesses KSAs related to team leadership effectiveness
- Individual teamwork contributes to a team's success
- Variability within a team has an additive effect on team effectiveness
- Helps you to assess how you contribute to a team's overall success
- Developmental, not evaluative
- Underlying approach is based on the experiential learning cycle- assess, reflect, plan, and take action

22 | •

Strategies for Leaders

1. TEAM CONTRACT

The act of writing a contract together as a team allows for attention to all of the components that we have addressed. A contract is a formal agreement that the team discusses and writes, with all of the team members signing to symbolize their agreement. The terms of the contract usually include the following components:

- What goals they plan on accomplishing on the team *(goals)*

- Who occupies specific roles necessary for team success and when they will rotate these roles *(roles)*

- How they will build opportunities for mastery into their project; how they will know what small and large successes are *(confidence)*

- The strengths of each team member and how team members will cover for each other in an unforeseen circumstance *(interpersonal understanding)*

- Team norms or rules around what constitutes appropriate behavior; this might include defining what respectful behavior is and is not *(psychological safety)*

- How work and knowledge will be coordinated; sharing of knowledge and resources *(coordination)*

- A timeframe for reevaluation of the contract, the purpose of the team, the goals of the team, the roles, etc. *(continuous improvement)*

- Specific measures on how to build change into the team and when to incorporate outside expertise and information *(adapting)*

2. OTHER STRATEGIES

- **Building Goals:** Write a team charter that explains the purpose and goals of the team. The document should include the expectations and goals of individual team members.

- **Building Roles:** Clarify who is responsible for each task and when it will be due to the team.

- **Building Team Confidence:** Take stock of team successes to date, identify experiences in past teams that were successful, and set short-term, easy-to-accomplish goals at first.

- **Psychological Safety:** Take time in each meeting to gather opinions of each member, seek out alternative viewpoints, and discuss weaknesses of the current position.

- **Interpersonal Understanding:** Begin each meeting with a brief "check in." For example, each person might respond to a question such as *How are you doing today?* or *What else is on your schedule?* or *Do you have anything that might be occupying your mind at this moment?*

- **Coordination:** Establish preset meeting times. Decide when specific tasks are due. Exchange cell phone numbers and e-mail addresses in case there is a change of plans or later questions.

- **Continuous Improvement:** Reserve no less that 5% of your time in meetings to discuss how things are going. Ask questions such as *What do we do well?* or *How might we improve on our work?* After particularly heated or conflict-ridden meetings, take more time and be sure to ask how the team can do things differently next time.

- **Adapting:** Establish a "turnaround time," in other words, reserve a time for reevaluation of the current goals or objectives. *Do we need to reexamine our goals? Do we have the right people on the project? Will we have access to all the resources we initially planned? Do we have a plan B in case we need to change our direction?*

FURTHER READING

Bailey, J. , Sass, M , Swiercz, P. M. , Seal, C. , & Kayes. D. C. 2005. Teaching with and through teams. Student-written, instructor-facilitated case writing and the signatory code. Journal of Management Education, 29, 1, 39-59.

Druskat, V. U. , & Kayes, D. C. 1999. The antecedents of team competence: Toward a fine-grained model of self-managing team effectiveness. In (Eds.), M. Neale and E. Mannix, Research on Teams and Teams, Vol. 2. JAI Press: Greenwich, CT.

Druskat, V. U. , & Kayes, D. C. 2000. Learning versus performance in short term project teams. Small Team Research, 31, 3, 328-353.

Kayes, D. C. , & Burnett, G. 2007. Team learning. In (Eds), J. Bailey & S. Clegg. International Encyclopedia of Organization Studies. Sage Publications.

Kayes, D. C. 2006. Destructive Goal Pursuit: The Mt. Everest Disaster. Palgrave- Macmillan.

Kayes, D. C. , & Kayes, A. B. 2006. Learning style composition in teams: Implications for assessment. In (Eds.) Sims, R. & Sims, E. Learning Styles and Learning: A Key to Meeting the Accountability Demands in Education. Nova Press.

Kayes, A. B. , Kayes, D. C. , & Kolb, D. A. 2005. Experiential learning in teams. Simulation & Gaming, 36, 3, 330-354.

Kayes, D. C. , & Kayes, A. B. 2011. The Learning Advantage: The six practices of learning directed leaders. Palgrave-Macmillan.

Kayes, D. C. 2009. The problem with performance: Conditions for team learning. In (Eds.) P. Kamur, P. Ramsey, & B. Mackie, Learning and Performance Matters. World Scientific Publishing Company.

Kayes. D. C. 2002. Conversational learning in organization and human resource development. In A. Baker, P. Jensen & D. Kolb (Eds.), Conversational learning: An experiential approach to knowledge creation. Westport, CT: Quorum Books.

Knott, M. Team learning. Unpublished doctoral dissertation. The George Washington University.

Web Resources

www.learningdirectedleadership.com

www.learningfromexperience.com

26 | •